Our Favo
RECIPES U
400 Calories

Copyright 2018, Gooseberry Patch
Previously published under ISBN 978-1-62093-031-1
Cover: California Pita Sandwiches (page 59)

Lighten Up!

Make a few easy changes for healthy, tasty meals your family will love.

- Farmers' markets are bursting with delicious fruits and vegetables. For the healthiest selection, choose a rainbow of colors...yellow peppers, red strawberries, orange sweet potatoes, purple cabbage, bright green zucchini. You'll be adding eye appeal too!

- Look for leaner cuts of beef, chicken and pork, and trim off visible fat before cooking.

- Choose stronger flavored versions of favorite ingredients, such as extra-sharp Cheddar cheese and Italian-seasoned diced tomatoes. You'll be adding flavor without adding calories.

- Olive oil and canola oil are higher in heart-healthy fats than other vegetable oils. When sautéing or pan-frying, cut calories by spraying the pan with non-stick vegetable spray instead of cooking in oil.

- Whole-grain pastas and flour add fiber to your diet...oats, brown rice and barley are delicious choices too. Sprinkle wheat germ or flax seed into baked goods for extra fiber and a nutty taste.

- Substitute margarine for butter, if you like. While "light" butters and margarines aren't meant for baking, it's easy to reduce fat in baked treats...just replace the oil in a recipe with an equal amount of applesauce.

Fresh herbs give a wonderful flavor boost! If a recipe
calls for one teaspoon of a dried herb, simply substitute
one tablespoon of the fresh herb. For best flavor,
add them toward the end of the cooking time.

Inside-Out Cabbage Rolls

Makes 6 servings at
220 calories each

1 lb. extra lean ground beef
1 onion, chopped
1 green pepper, chopped
10-oz. can diced tomatoes and
    green chiles
1 head cabbage, chopped

1 c. beef broth
8-oz. can pizza sauce
1 c. cooked brown rice
1/2 c. shredded reduced-fat
    Cheddar cheese

In a Dutch oven over medium heat, cook beef, onion and green pepper until beef is no longer pink; drain. Stir in tomatoes with juice, cabbage, broth and pizza sauce. Bring to a boil; reduce heat to low. Cover and simmer for 20 to 25 minutes, until cabbage is tender, stirring occasionally. Stir in rice; heat through. Remove from heat. Sprinkle with cheese; cover and let stand until cheese is melted.

Set a pretty place for dinner with a lacy napkin, a few blooms
in a tiny vase and a salad plate instead of a dinner plate.
Your portions will seem larger.

Veggie-Stuffed Peppers

Makes 4 servings at
210 calories each

1 c. vegetable broth
1 c. sliced mushrooms
2/3 c. quick-cooking barley,
    uncooked
2 green peppers, halved
    lengthwise and seeded
3/4 c. shredded reduced-fat
    mozzarella cheese, divided

1 egg, beaten
3/4 c. tomato, chopped
1/2 c. zucchini, shredded
1/3 c. soft bread crumbs
1/2 t. dried basil
1/8 t. dried rosemary
1/8 t. onion salt

In a saucepan over medium-high heat, combine broth, mushrooms and barley. Bring to a boil; reduce heat to low. Cover and simmer for 12 to 15 minutes, until barley is tender. Drain well. Meanwhile, fill a separate saucepan with water and bring to a boil. Add pepper halves and boil for 3 minutes; drain on paper towels. In a bowl, stir together barley mixture, 1/2 cup cheese and remaining ingredients. Arrange pepper halves in an ungreased 2-quart casserole dish; fill with barley mixture. Cover and bake at 350 degrees for 20 to 25 minutes, until tender and heated through. Sprinkle remaining cheese over peppers. Return to oven until cheese melts, about 2 minutes.

Bake a quiche in muffin or custard cups for oh-so simple
portion control. When making minis, reduce the baking time
by about 10 minutes, and slide a toothpick into each
to check for doneness.

Crustless Spinach Quiche

*Makes 6 servings at
230 calories each*

10-oz. pkg. frozen chopped
    spinach, thawed and
    squeezed dry
16-oz. container reduced-fat
    small-curd cottage cheese
3 eggs, beaten

1/4 c. butter, melted
1 c. shredded reduced-fat
    Cheddar cheese
1 t. salt
1/2 t. pepper

In a large bowl, mix all ingredients until well blended. Pour into a
greased 8" pie plate. Bake, uncovered, at 325 degrees for one hour, or
until set. Cut into wedges to serve.

To freshen cooking pans after preparing fish in them, simply fill
the pan with equal parts vinegar and water. Bring to a boil for
5 minutes, let cool, then wash the pan with hot, soapy water.

Tomato-Mushroom Grilled Fish

*Makes 4 servings at
300 calories each*

2 T. butter, softened
8 c. baby spinach
1-1/2 lbs. orange roughy fillets,
    1/2-inch thick
salt and pepper to taste
1 c. zucchini, cut into thin strips

8 mushrooms, sliced
2 tomatoes, chopped
1/2 c. fresh basil, chopped
1/4 c. lime juice
2 T. olive oil

Lay out four 15-inch pieces of heavy-duty aluminum foil. Spread butter down the center of each piece. Lay 2 cups spinach on buttered area of each piece. Place fish on top; season with salt and pepper. Divide zucchini, mushrooms and tomato evenly over fish. Sprinkle with basil; drizzle with lime juice and olive oil. To seal, fold one long edge of foil over the other; tuck short ends underneath, making tightly wrapped packages. Place packages on a baking sheet. Bake at 450 degrees for 15 to 18 minutes, until fish flakes easily with a fork. Serve fish with vegetables.

Reduced-fat dairy products like shredded cheese, sour cream, cream cheese and milk are an easy substitute for their full-fat counterparts in recipes. Flavor and texture may vary from brand to brand...you're sure to find some that you like just as much as the "real thing."

Cheesy Ham & Vegetable Bake

*Makes 6 servings at
270 calories each*

1-1/2 c. rotini pasta, uncooked
16-oz. pkg. frozen broccoli,
    carrots and cauliflower blend
1/2 c. reduced-fat sour cream
1/2 c. low-fat milk
1-1/2 c. cooked ham, chopped

1-1/2 c. shredded reduced-fat
    Cheddar cheese, divided
1/4 c. onion, chopped
1 clove garlic, minced
1/2 c. croutons, crushed

Cook pasta according to package directions; add frozen vegetables to cooking water to thaw. Drain; place mixture in a 2-quart casserole dish sprayed with non-stick vegetable spray. Mix sour cream, milk, ham, one cup cheese, onion and garlic; stir into pasta mixture in dish. Bake, uncovered, at 350 degrees for 25 minutes. Sprinkle with croutons and remaining cheese; return to oven for 5 minutes, or until cheese melts.

For a delicious low-calorie change from pasta, make "noodles"
from zucchini or summer squash. Cut into long, thin strips,
steam lightly or sauté in a little olive oil and toss
with your favorite pasta sauce.

Grandma's Spaghetti Supreme

Makes 8 servings at
390 calories each

16-oz. pkg. spaghetti, uncooked
1 lb. extra lean ground beef
1/4 c. onion, chopped
2 10-3/4 oz. cans tomato soup

10-3/4 oz. can fat-free cream of
    mushroom soup
1 c. shredded reduced-fat Cheddar
    cheese

Cook spaghetti according to package directions; drain. Meanwhile,
in a large skillet over medium heat, brown beef and onion; drain.
Add tomato soup and spaghetti; mix together. Transfer to a greased
13"x9" baking pan. Spoon mushroom soup over top. Bake, uncovered,
at 350 degrees for about 40 minutes, until bubbly around the edges.
Sprinkle with cheese and return to oven until cheese is melted, about
5 minutes.

Place browned ground beef or turkey in a colander and
run hot water over it. Excess fat will rinse right off
with no loss in flavor.

Slow-Cooker Beef & Bean Burritos

Makes 12 burritos at 370 calories each

2-lb. lean beef flank steak
1-1/4 oz. pkg. taco seasoning mix
1 c. sweet onion, chopped
1 T. cider vinegar
4-1/2 oz. can chopped green
   chiles

16-oz. can fat-free refried beans
12 8-inch flour tortillas
1-1/2 c. shredded reduced-fat
   Monterey Jack cheese
1-1/2 c. roma tomatoes, chopped
3/4 c. reduced-fat sour cream

Trim any fat from beef; rub all sides with taco seasoning. Place beef in a slow cooker that has been sprayed with non-stick vegetable spray. Add onion, vinegar and chiles to slow cooker. Cover and cook on low setting for 8 to 9 hours, until beef is very tender. Remove beef from slow cooker; shred with 2 forks and return to slow cooker. Warm beans according to package directions. Spread 2 tablespoons of beans in the center of each tortilla. Top beans with 1/3 cup of beef mixture. Sprinkle with cheese and tomatoes; dollop with a tablespoon of sour cream. Roll up tightly.

A flexible plastic cutting mat makes speedy work of slicing & dicing. Keep two mats on hand for chopping meat and veggies separately.

Orange Chicken Italiano

Makes 4 servings at
200 calories each

1 lb. boneless, skinless chicken
    breasts
1 c. orange juice
1/2 c. chicken broth
1-1/2 t. Italian seasoning

paprika to taste
1 onion, chopped
1 tomato, chopped
1-1/2 c. sliced mushrooms
2 t. olive oil

Place chicken in a lightly greased shallow casserole dish. Combine orange juice and broth in a bowl; drizzle over chicken. Sprinkle with seasonings. Bake, uncovered, at 350 degrees for 30 minutes. Meanwhile, in a skillet over medium heat, sauté vegetables in oil until tender, 5 to 7 minutes. Spoon vegetables over chicken. Return to oven and bake, uncovered, for 30 additional minutes, or until chicken juices run clear when pierced.

Non-stick vegetable spray is a terrific way to save both
time and calories when fixing a stir-fried or sautéed recipe.
Look for olive oil spray for added flavor.

Skinny Italian Creamy Chicken

Makes 4 servings at 358 calories each, excluding optional rice or pasta

4 boneless, skinless chicken breasts
.7-oz. pkg. Italian salad dressing mix
1/3 c. warm water
8-oz. pkg. reduced-fat cream cheese, softened

1/2 c. plain non-fat yogurt
10-3/4 oz. can fat-free cream of chicken soup
1/2 c. shredded Parmesan cheese
Optional: cooked rice or pasta

Place chicken in a lightly greased slow cooker. In a small bowl, whisk together salad dressing mix and water; pour over chicken. In a separate bowl, beat together cream cheese, yogurt and soup; spoon over chicken. Sprinkle with Parmesan cheese. Cover and cook on low setting for 6 to 8 hours, until chicken juices run clear. Serve over rice or pasta, if desired.

Don't fall back on fast food when you're short on time! Take a
weekend to prepare several good-for-you casseroles and
dinners to tuck in the freezer for future use.

Kim's Crustless Pizza

*Makes 8 servings at
300 calories each,
excluding optional toppings*

2 lbs. extra-lean ground beef
garlic salt and pepper to taste
2 t. dried, minced onion
2 c. shredded reduced-fat
    mozzarella cheese
16-oz. jar pizza sauce
1 c. shredded reduced-fat
    Italian-blend cheese

3-1/2 oz. pkg. sliced turkey
    pepperoni
Optional: sliced mushrooms,
    banana pepper rings, chopped
    tomato, onion, green pepper

Brown beef with seasonings and onion in a skillet over medium heat;
drain. In a bowl, stir together beef mixture and mozzarella cheese. Spread
beef mixture evenly in an ungreased 17"x11" jelly-roll pan. Top beef
mixture with pizza sauce, Italian-blend cheese and desired toppings.
Bake at 350 degrees for 25 minutes, or until beef is no longer pink and
cheese is melted. Let stand 5 minutes; cut into squares to serve.

Keep a chilled pitcher of water in the fridge for a refreshing thirst quencher anytime. Dress it up with a few lemon wedges, orange slices or sprigs of fresh mint.

Deb's Chicken Florentine

Makes 6 servings at 400 calories each

16-oz. pkg. linguine pasta,
    uncooked and divided
1 T. olive oil
3 cloves garlic, minced
4 boneless, skinless chicken
    breasts, thinly sliced
1-1/4 c. fat-free zesty Italian
    salad dressing, divided

8 sun-dried tomatoes, chopped
8-oz. pkg. sliced mushrooms
5-oz. pkg. baby spinach
cracked pepper to taste
Garnish: chopped fresh parsley

Cook 3/4 of pasta according to package directions; set aside. Reserve remaining pasta for another recipe. While pasta is cooking, warm oil in a skillet over medium heat. Add garlic and cook 2 minutes. Add chicken; cook until no longer pink in the center. Drizzle chicken with one cup salad dressing. Stir in tomatoes and mushrooms; cover skillet and simmer until mushrooms are softened. Add spinach; cover skillet again. Cook another 2 to 3 minutes, just until spinach is wilted; stir and sprinkle with pepper. Toss cooked linguine with remaining salad dressing. Serve chicken and vegetables over linguine, garnished with parsley.

Sliced mushrooms add savory flavor and extra bulk,
but few calories. Feel free to add them generously
to casseroles, stir-fries and pizza.

26

Grilled Veggies & Sausage

*Makes 6 servings at
290 calories each*

1 lb. smoked turkey sausage,
   cut into bite-size pieces
4 redskin potatoes, cubed
16-oz. pkg. baby carrots
1 yellow squash, cut into
   1-inch cubes

1 zucchini, cut into 1-inch cubes
1/2 c. red onion, thinly sliced
2 T. olive oil
salt, pepper, minced garlic, dried
   parsley and Italian seasoning
   to taste

Arrange sausage and vegetables on a long piece of heavy-duty
aluminum foil coated with non-stick vegetable spray. Drizzle with oil.
Sprinkle with desired seasonings. Seal edges of foil tightly to create a
foil pack. Place on a heated grill and cook for about one hour, until all
vegetables are tender.

Chicken thighs are juicy, flavorful and similar in calories
to boneless chicken breasts. Speed up cooking time by using
a sharp knife to make a deep cut on each side of the bone.

28

Spicy Glazed Chicken & Barley

Makes 6 servings at 170 calories each

6 skinless chicken thighs
2 T. soy sauce
2 t. honey
2 t. spicy brown mustard
14-1/2 oz. can chicken broth with
    roasted vegetables

3/4 c. quick-cooking barley,
    uncooked
1/2 c. frozen petite peas
salt and pepper to taste

Arrange chicken in a lightly greased 13"x9" baking pan. Whisk together soy sauce, honey and mustard; brush half of mixture over chicken. Bake, uncovered, at 375 degrees for 15 minutes. Turn chicken over; brush with remaining soy sauce mixture. Bake an additional 15 minutes, or until chicken is golden and juices run clear. Meanwhile, bring broth to a boil in a saucepan over medium heat. Stir in uncooked barley. Reduce heat; cover and simmer for 5 minutes. Add remaining ingredients to barley. Cook an additional 5 to 7 minutes, until barley is tender and liquid is absorbed. Slice chicken; serve with barley.

Skillet stir-fries are a versatile way to prepare a healthy veggie-packed meal. Try using sliced pork, beef or chicken, or make it a meatless meal. Add any fresh vegetables you have on hand...tomato, green pepper and celery are tasty!

Chicken Stir-Fry

Makes 6 servings at
150 calories each

1 t. soy sauce
2 T. apple juice
1/8 t. ground ginger
1/2 t. salt
pepper to taste
1/2 lb. boneless, skinless chicken
  breast, thinly sliced
1/4 c. peanut oil, divided

3 c. snow peas
1/2 c. celery, thinly sliced
5-oz. can sliced bamboo shoots,
  drained
1/2 c. green onions, thinly sliced
1/2 c. sliced mushrooms
1 c. chicken broth

In a bowl, whisk together soy sauce, juice and seasonings. Add chicken
and turn to coat; let marinate 5 minutes. Heat 2 tablespoons oil in a large
skillet over high heat. Stirring constantly, cook chicken mixture in oil for
5 minutes, or until cooked through. Remove chicken mixture and keep
warm. Add remaining oil to skillet; stir in vegetables and broth. Cook
over high heat for 5 minutes, stirring constantly. Add chicken mixture
to skillet and cook an additional 5 minutes, stirring constantly.

If you have formed the habit of checking on every new diet
that comes along, you will find that, mercifully, they all blur
together, leaving you with only one definite piece
of information: French-fried potatoes are out.

—Jean Kerr

Rosemary Pork Loin

*Makes 4 servings at
160 calories each*

1 T. butter
1-lb. pork tenderloin, sliced
   one-inch thick
1 c. sliced mushrooms
2 T. onion, finely chopped

1-1/2 T. fresh rosemary, chopped
1 clove garlic, minced
salt and pepper to taste
1 T. apple juice
Garnish: fresh rosemary sprigs

Melt butter in a heavy skillet over medium-high heat. Brown pork slices quickly, about one minute on each side. Remove pork to a serving plate, reserving drippings in skillet. Add remaining ingredients except juice and garnish to skillet. Cook and stir over low heat for several minutes, or until mushrooms and onion are almost tender. Stir in juice. Return pork to skillet; spoon mushroom mixture over pork. Cover; simmer 3 to 4 more minutes. Garnish with sprigs of rosemary.

For hearty salads in a snap, keep unopened cans of diced tomatoes, black olives, white beans and artichoke hearts in the fridge. They'll be chilled and ready to toss with fresh greens at a moment's notice.

Pasta Primavera Even Kids Like
Makes 6 servings at 290 calories each

12-oz. pkg. whole-wheat linguine
    pasta, uncooked
1 T. olive oil
3 cloves garlic, minced
1 red pepper, cut into strips
1/2 lb. asparagus, trimmed
    and sliced
1 c. cherry tomatoes, halved
1 c. sliced mushrooms

1 T. all-purpose flour
1 c. chicken broth
1/2 c. low-fat milk
1/2 t. salt
1/2 t. pepper
2 carrots, peeled and cut into
    ribbons with peeler
Garnish: 2 T. grated Parmesan
    cheese

Cook pasta according to package directions. Drain, reserving 1/2 cup of pasta water. Meanwhile, heat oil in a large skillet over medium-high heat. Add garlic; cook and stir for one minute. Add red pepper; cook and stir until it begins to soften, about 3 minutes. Add asparagus, tomatoes and mushrooms; cook until tender. Stir in flour; cook and stir for one minute. Add broth, milk, salt and pepper; bring to a boil. Reduce heat. Cook until liquid thickens slightly, about 5 minutes. Stir in carrots. Toss pasta with sauce and vegetables, adding reserved water as necessary to moisten. Sprinkle with cheese.

Be a savvy shopper. Group items on your shopping list by
the area of the store where they're found...fruits and
vegetables, meat, dairy and frozen foods. You'll find it
much easier to stick to a healthy meal plan.

Spicy Pork Noodle Bowls

*Makes 4 servings at
300 calories each*

8-oz. pkg. whole-wheat linguine
    pasta, uncooked and divided
2 T. canola oil, divided
1 lb. boneless pork shoulder,
    sliced into strips
1 onion, thinly sliced

1/2 lb. broccoli flowerets
2 T. Worcestershire sauce
1 T. soy sauce
2 t. cornstarch
1/2 t. curry powder
1 tomato, chopped

Cook half of pasta according to package directions; set aside. Reserve
remaining pasta for another recipe. Meanwhile, heat one tablespoon oil
in a large skillet over high heat. Add pork; cook and stir until golden,
about 7 minutes. Remove pork; set aside. Heat remaining oil in skillet;
add onion and broccoli. Cook and stir until tender, about 5 minutes. Mix
together sauces, cornstarch and curry powder in a cup; stir into skillet.
Cook and stir until slightly thickened. Return pork to pan; heat through.
Divide cooked pasta into 4 shallow bowls. Top with pork mixture and
tomato; toss to coat pasta.

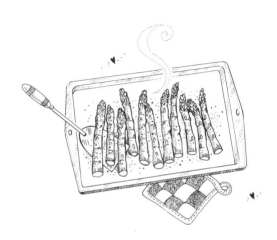

A delicious no-fuss side...tuck some roasted vegetables into the oven along with a main-dish casserole. Toss peeled, sliced veggies with a little olive oil and spread on a baking sheet. Bake at 350 degrees, stirring occasionally, for 15 to 25 minutes, until tender and golden.

Basil & Tomato Halibut

Makes 6 servings at 190 calories each, excluding optional rice

1 T. olive oil
1 t. butter
1 onion, sliced
4 cloves garlic, minced
8 roma tomatoes, diced
14-1/2 oz. can chicken broth

1 t. seafood seasoning
salt and pepper to taste
2 lbs. halibut fillets
3 T. fresh basil, chopped
Optional: cooked rice

Heat oil and butter in a skillet over medium heat. Add onion and garlic. Sauté for 3 minutes; stir in tomatoes, broth and seasonings. Add fish to skillet. Reduce heat to medium-low. Cover and cook until fish flakes easily, about 8 minutes. Remove fish from sauce to a plate. Add basil to sauce in skillet; stir and spoon over fish and rice, if using.

Here's a handy tip to make frozen fish taste fresh and mild...
just place the frozen fillets in a shallow dish, cover with
milk and thaw in the refrigerator overnight.

Tilapia with Dill Sauce

*Makes 4 servings of fish
& sauce at 190 calories each*

1 lb. tilapia fillets
1-1/2 t. Cajun seasoning

salt and pepper to taste
1 lemon, thinly sliced

Prepare Dill Sauce; let stand while preparing fish to allow flavors to blend. Sprinkle both sides of fish with seasonings. Arrange in a single layer in a lightly greased 13"x9" baking pan. Arrange lemon slices evenly over fish. Bake, uncovered, at 350 degrees for 15 to 20 minutes, until fish flakes easily with a fork. Top fish with Dill Sauce.

Dill Sauce:

1/2 c. reduced-fat sour cream
1/4 c. reduced-fat mayonnaise
1/8 t. garlic powder

1 t. lemon juice
2 T. fresh dill, chopped

Blend all ingredients in a small bowl. May be prepared ahead of time and refrigerated.

After dinner, take a nature hike around the neighborhood.
Take along a pocket-size nature guide, a magnifying glass
and a tote bag to bring back special finds. Fun for
young & old, and a great way to get a little exercise.

Slow-Cooker Harvest Stew

*Makes 6 servings at
370 calories each*

1 lb. lean ground turkey
1 acorn squash
14-1/2 oz. can diced tomatoes
16-oz. can kidney beans, drained
    and rinsed
3 redskin potatoes, peeled
    and chopped

1 sweet potato, peeled
    and chopped
1 yellow onion, chopped
3 cloves garlic, chopped
4 c. chicken broth

In a skillet over medium heat, brown turkey; drain and set aside.
Microwave whole squash on high setting for 2 minutes; peel and cube.
Add squash, turkey, tomatoes with juice and remaining ingredients to
a large slow cooker; stir well. Cover and cook on low setting for
7 to 9 hours.

Make your own nutritious vegetable broth. Place veggie scraps and trimmings in a soup pot, add water to cover and simmer gently for 30 minutes. Strain and use to make soup or freeze in ice cube trays to add extra flavor to recipes.

Asian Chicken Soup

Makes 4 servings at
210 calories

3 14-1/2 oz. cans chicken broth
2 c. water
1 T. fresh ginger, peeled and
    grated
1 clove garlic, slivered
1/4 t. red pepper flakes
8-oz. pkg. whole-wheat spaghetti,
    uncooked and divided

2 boneless, skinless chicken
    breasts, thinly sliced
1 red pepper, thinly sliced
1 c. snow peas, chopped
juice of 1 lime
2 green onions, thinly sliced
salt to taste

In a large soup pot over high heat, bring broth, water, ginger, garlic and red pepper flakes to a boil. Add half of the uncooked spaghetti, reserving the rest for another recipe. Reduce heat; simmer until spaghetti is tender, about 6 to 8 minutes. Add chicken, pepper and snow peas. Simmer until chicken juices run clear, about 3 minutes. Stir in lime juice, green onions and salt.

Give whole-wheat pasta a try! While the calorie count is about the same as regular pasta, it contains more fiber for an easy nutrition boost. Check the label to be sure it's made with whole-wheat flour, not simply wheat flour.

Pasta e Fagioli

Makes 6 servings at
340 calories each

15-oz. can cannellini beans
2 T. olive oil
3 slices turkey bacon, coarsely
    chopped
2 stalks celery, chopped
2 carrots, peeled and chopped
1 onion, chopped
2 cloves garlic, minced

3 14-1/2 oz. cans chicken broth
15-oz. can kidney beans, drained
    and rinsed
1 c. small shell pasta, uncooked
salt and pepper to taste
Garnish: 6 T. grated Parmesan
    cheese

Mash undrained cannellini beans with a fork and set aside. In a
saucepan, heat oil over medium heat; add bacon, celery, carrots, onion
and garlic. Cook for 7 to 10 minutes, stirring occasionally, until bacon
is crisp and vegetables are softened. Add broth, cannellini beans and
kidney beans; bring to a boil over high heat. Stir in pasta. Reduce heat
to medium. Cook, uncovered, for 6 to 8 minutes, stirring frequently, until
pasta is tender. Season with salt and pepper. Ladle into soup bowls; top
each bowl with a tablespoon of cheese.

Start dinner with a cup of hot soup...it's sure to
take the edge off your appetite.

Fishermen's Stew

*Makes 6 servings at
320 calories each*

2 t. olive oil
2 c. smoked turkey sausage, diced
2 c. onions, chopped
4 c. chicken broth
8-oz. bottle clam juice
2 6-oz. cans chopped clams
1 lb. cod or halibut, cut into
    1-inch cubes

15-oz. can chickpeas, drained
    and rinsed
1 sweet potato, peeled and diced
1 bay leaf
2 t. lemon juice
1/4 t. pepper

Heat oil in a large saucepan. Add sausage and onions; stir until onions
soften. Stir in remaining ingredients except lemon juice and pepper.
Simmer until fish flakes easily and sweet potato is tender, about
10 minutes. Discard bay leaf; stir in lemon juice and pepper.

To create a thick, creamy vegetable or bean soup without
adding any cream, use a hand-held immersion blender to
purée some of the cooked veggies right in the saucepan.

Chill-Chaser Pork Stew

*Makes 6 servings at
350 calories each*

2 lbs. boneless pork steaks, cubed
2 T. olive oil
2 sweet onions, chopped
2 green peppers, chopped
2 cloves garlic, minced

salt and pepper to taste
6-oz. can tomato paste
28-oz. can diced tomatoes
2 8-oz. cans sliced mushrooms,
    drained

In a Dutch oven over medium heat, sauté pork in oil until browned. Add onions, green peppers, garlic, salt and pepper. Cover; cook over medium heat until pork is tender. Add tomato paste, tomatoes with juice and mushrooms; bring to a boil. Reduce heat to low; cover and simmer for one hour, stirring often.

A ridged cast-iron grill skillet is handy for grilling
on your stovetop whenever it's too cold or rainy
to use the grill outdoors.

Raspberry-Dijon Chicken Baguettes

*Makes 4 sandwiches at
380 calories each*

4 boneless, skinless chicken
    breasts
4 mini baguette rolls, halved
    lengthwise
8 t. Dijon mustard

8 t. no-sugar-added raspberry
    spread
1-1/2 c. fresh arugula, torn
4 thin slices red onion

Broil or grill chicken until golden and juices run clear; slice. Spread
bottom half of baguettes with mustard; spread top half with raspberry
spread. Layer grilled chicken over mustard; top with arugula and onion.
Add top half of baguettes.

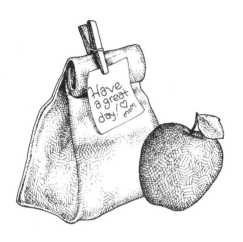

A healthy light wrap for smaller appetites! Simply layer
sandwich toppings on lettuce leaves instead of bread,
roll up and enjoy.

Mom's Eggplant Sandwich

*Makes 6 servings at
320 calories each*

1 eggplant, peeled and sliced
    1/2-inch thick
2 zucchini or yellow squash,
    sliced 1/2-inch thick
salt and pepper to taste
2 T. olive oil

1/4 c. reduced-fat mayonnaise
1 French baguette loaf, halved
    lengthwise
1 tomato, thinly sliced
1/4 c. grated Parmesan cheese,
    divided

Sprinkle eggplant and squash slices with salt and pepper; set aside. Heat oil in a grill pan over medium heat. Grill eggplant and squash until veggies are tender and have grill marks; drain on a paper towel. Spread mayonnaise over cut sides of loaf. Arrange tomato slices on bottom half; sprinkle with salt, pepper and half of Parmesan cheese. Layer grilled eggplant and squash over tomatoes. Sprinkle with remaining cheese and add top half; slice into 6 pieces.

For the best results when using reduced-fat cheese, use very low heat, as high heat causes it to toughen. Reserve fat-free cheese for use in cold dishes like salads and deli sandwiches.

Toasty Ham & Swiss Stacks

Makes 4 servings at
370 calories each

2 T. reduced-fat mayonnaise
4 t. Dijon mustard
2 t. fresh dill, finely chopped
salt and pepper to taste
1 lb. sliced mushrooms

2 T. olive oil
8 slices rye bread, toasted
4 slices deli ham
4 slices reduced-fat Swiss cheese
4 thin slices red onion

In a small bowl, whisk together mayonnaise, mustard, dill, salt and pepper; set aside. In a skillet over medium-high heat, sauté mushrooms in oil, stirring occasionally, for 5 minutes, or until liquid evaporates. Remove from heat; drain. Spread 4 toast slices with mayonnaise mixture. Layer each slice with ham, mushrooms, cheese and onion. Place on an ungreased baking sheet. Broil under a preheated broiler, about 4 inches from heat, for one to 2 minutes, until lightly golden and cheese is melted. Top with remaining toast slices.

Use mustard instead of mayonnaise on sandwiches
for a big saving in calories.

California Pita Sandwiches

Makes 2 servings
194 calories each

1 whole-grain pita round, halved
  and split
1/2 avocado, halved, pitted and
  sliced
1 tomato, sliced

1 slice reduced-fat Swiss cheese,
  halved
4 leaves Bibb lettuce
2 t. Thousand Island salad
  dressing

Fill each half of pita with avocado, tomato, cheese, lettuce leaves and
dressing. Serve immediately.

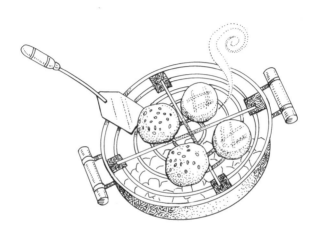

Grill or toast buns slightly before adding shredded or
sliced meat...it only takes a minute and makes
such a tasty difference!

Grilled Salmon BLTs

*Makes 4 sandwiches at
390 calories each*

1/3 c. reduced-fat mayonnaise
2 t. fresh dill, chopped
1 t. lemon zest
1 lb. salmon fillets, cut into
    4 pieces
1/4 t. salt

1/8 t. pepper
8 thin slices white bread
4 romaine lettuce leaves
2 tomatoes, sliced
4 thin slices turkey bacon, crisply
    cooked and halved

Stir together mayonnaise, dill and zest in a small bowl; set aside. Sprinkle salmon with salt and pepper; place on a lightly greased hot grill, skin-side down. Cover and cook for about 10 to 12 minutes, without turning, until cooked through. Slide a thin metal spatula between salmon and skin; lift salmon and transfer to plate. Discard skin. Arrange bread slices on grill; toast lightly on both sides. Spread 4 bread slices on one side with mayonnaise mixture. Top each slice with one lettuce leaf, 2 tomato slices, one salmon fillet, 2 pieces bacon and remaining bread slice.

Keep bags of sweetened dried cranberries and chopped walnuts
tucked in the cupboard for healthy between-meal snacking.
A quick toss of nuts & berries really dresses up a
plain-Jane salad in a snap too.

Sandra's Pomegranate Salad

*Makes 6 servings at
170 calories each*

6 c. fresh arugula, torn
2 ripe pears, halved, cored and
    cut into wedges
2 T. olive oil
2 T. lime juice
1/2 t. Dijon mustard

salt and pepper to taste
seeds of 1 pomegranate
1/2 c. crumbled feta cheese
1/3 c. toasted chopped pecans
Garnish: Boston or Bibb lettuce
    leaves

Place arugula and pears in a large salad bowl; set aside. In a small bowl,
whisk together olive oil, lime juice and mustard. Toss arugula and pears
with desired amount of oil mixture; season with salt and pepper. Sprinkle
salad with remaining ingredients except lettuce leaves and toss gently.
Line 6 salad plates with lettuce leaves; top each plate with a serving
of salad.

Fresh fruit salad is a scrumptious, healthy side that just about everyone will love. Cut two to three kinds of seasonal fruit into cubes and toss with a simple dressing made of equal parts honey and lemon or orange juice.

Simple Coleslaw

Makes 6 servings at
110 calories each

1 head cabbage, chopped
4 carrots, peeled and grated
1 onion, chopped
8-oz. can sliced pineapple,
    drained and chopped

1 c. plain non-fat yogurt
salt and pepper to taste
Optional: garlic powder and
    paprika to taste

In a large serving bowl, mix cabbage, carrots, onion, pineapple and yogurt. Stir in desired seasonings. Cover and chill for 30 minutes before serving.

Salad smarts! The darker the greens, the healthier they are for you. Try spinach or romaine lettuce...if iceberg lettuce is more to your liking, try a mix of iceberg and darker greens.

Quick & Easy Veggie Salad

*Makes 6 servings at
40 calories each*

1/2 head cauliflower, chopped
1 bunch broccoli, chopped
1 tomato, chopped

1/4 c. red onion, sliced
1/4 c. fat-free Italian salad
  dressing

Combine cauliflower, broccoli, tomato and onion in a serving bowl.
Drizzle with dressing; toss to mix. Serve immediately, or chill until ready
to serve.

Light olive oil is budget-friendly and is fine for sautéing and baking...save rich-tasting extra-virgin olive oil for delicately flavored salad dressings and dipping sauces. Both kinds have the same calorie content.

68

White Bean & Tomato Salad

*Makes 6 servings at
140 calories each*

15-oz. can cannellini beans,
    drained and rinsed
2 zucchini or yellow squash, diced
1 pt. cherry tomatoes, halved

1/2 c. red onion, chopped
3 T. olive oil
2 T. lemon juice
1/4 c. fresh cilantro, chopped

Combine all ingredients in a large bowl; toss to coat. Cover and refrigerate
at least one hour. Let stand at room temperature 20 to 30 minutes
before serving.

Add zest to a tried & true recipe...easy! Just choose a seasoned variety of canned diced tomatoes like Italian or Mexican. The extra ingredients add few calories, but lots of flavor.

Minted Green Bean Salad

Makes 4 servings at
130 calories each

1-1/2 lbs. green beans, trimmed
1 t. garlic, minced
1/2 t. salt
1/4 c. white wine vinegar
2 T. lemon juice

pepper to taste
1/4 c. olive oil
2 T. fresh mint, minced
1 T. fresh basil, minced
1/2 c. red onion, finely chopped

In a stockpot of boiling water, cook beans for 3 to 5 minutes, until crisp-tender. Transfer beans to a large bowl of ice water to chill; drain well and set aside. Combine garlic and salt in a small bowl. Use the back of a spoon to crush garlic to a paste consistency. Add vinegar, lemon juice and pepper to garlic; whisk to blend. Add oil and herbs; whisk until well blended. In a serving bowl, combine beans and onion; toss with dressing to coat. Cover and chill 20 minutes before serving.

He who enjoys good health is rich,
though he knows it not.

— Italian Proverb

Mediterranean Couscous Salad
Makes 10 servings at 210 calories each

10-oz. pkg. couscous, uncooked
1/4 c. plus 1 T. olive oil, divided
1/2 c. lemon juice
1 t. Italian seasoning
15-1/2 oz. can black beans,
    drained and rinsed

6-oz. pkg. baby spinach
1 t. salt
1/2 t. pepper

Prepare couscous according to package directions; drain and set aside.
In a saucepan over medium heat, combine 1/4 cup oil, lemon juice and
Italian seasoning. Bring to a low boil; stir in beans and cook until
warmed through. Meanwhile, add remaining oil to a skillet over medium
heat; add spinach and cook until wilted. Add bean mixture to spinach
and stir gently. Stir in couscous, salt and pepper. Serve immediately, or
chill overnight and serve cold.

Check out a nearby farmers' market for seasonal, locally grown vegetables, fruit and herbs. It's a great place to save on fresh-picked produce...you may even discover a new favorite! Growers are happy to share free advice on selection and preparation.

Sunny Quinoa Salad

*Makes 8 servings at
250 calories each*

2 c. quinoa, uncooked
2-1/2 c. chicken broth
4 green onions, thinly sliced
1/2 c. golden raisins, chopped
2 T. rice vinegar
1/2 c. orange juice
1 t. orange zest

2 T. olive oil
1/4 t. ground cumin
1 cucumber, peeled and chopped
1/2 c. fresh flat-leaf parsley,
   chopped
salt and pepper to taste

Rinse quinoa under cold water until water runs clear. In a saucepan,
bring chicken broth to a boil over medium-high heat. Add quinoa; return
to a boil. Cover and simmer until quinoa has fully expanded, about 20 to
25 minutes. Remove from heat; fluff with a fork. In a large bowl,
combine quinoa and remaining ingredients; mix well. Cover and chill
before serving.

Iced tea is a refreshing beverage anytime! Simply place
two family-size teabags in a two-quart pitcher of cold water.
Refrigerate overnight to brew. Serve lightly sweetened
or unsweetened, garnished with lemon.

Italian Tomato Salad

3 tomatoes, cubed
1 T. fresh basil, chopped
1 T. olive oil
1 T. red wine vinegar

1/2 c. fat-free Italian salad
    dressing
4 slices Italian bread

In a salad bowl, mix together all ingredients. Cover and chill for at least
30 minutes. Toss again just before serving time. Garnish each serving
with a slice of bread to dip in the dressing.

Fat-free vinaigrette is so fresh-tasting on salad greens.
Fill a cruet bottle with 1/2 cup herb-flavored vinegar,
2 tablespoons water, one tablespoon Dijon mustard,
2 teaspoons Worcestershire sauce, 4 teaspoons sugar
or sweetener, 2 pressed garlic cloves and a dash
of pepper...shake and enjoy!

Tossed Salad & Cider Dressing

Makes 6 servings at 45 calories each

2 c. fresh spinach, torn
2 c. romaine lettuce, torn

1 c. iceberg lettuce, torn

Toss together spinach and lettuces in a salad bowl. Drizzle with desired amount of Cider Dressing; toss well and serve immediately.

Cider Dressing:

1/4 c. frozen apple juice
    concentrate, thawed
3 T. reduced-fat sour cream
3 T. water
2 T. cider vinegar
2 T. fresh parsley, chopped

2 T. apple, peeled, cored and
    finely shredded
1 T. Dijon mustard
1/4 t. salt
1/8 t. pepper

Whisk together all ingredients. Keep refrigerated; shake well before using.

Pack leftover veggie dishes into small containers for next day's lunch. Add a little sliced lean meat or some reduced-fat cheese cubes and you've got a delicious, healthy lunch all set to go.

My Favorite Greek Salad

*Makes 4 servings at
260 calories each*

1 cucumber, peeled and diced
2 tomatoes, diced
1/2 red onion, thinly sliced
1/2 c. pitted Kalamata olives
1/2 c. crumbled feta cheese

3 T. olive oil
2 T. lemon juice
1 t. dried oregano
1/8 t. salt
1/8 t. sugar

Combine vegetables and cheese in a large bowl. In a separate bowl,
whisk together remaining ingredients; toss gently with vegetable
mixture. Serve immediately, or chill until ready to serve.

Experimenting with healthy changes to your family's
favorite recipes? Try changing just one ingredient at a time...
a terrific way to learn which flavors you like. Don't forget
to add a note on your recipe card!

Country Veggie Bake

Makes 6 servings at
280 calories each

1 to 2 T. olive oil
2 carrots, peeled, halved
    lengthwise and sliced
2 onions, chopped
1 to 2 cloves garlic, chopped
1 c. mushrooms, quartered
15-oz. can black beans, drained
    and rinsed

14-oz. can vegetable or
    chicken broth
1 c. frozen corn
1/2 c. pearled barley, uncooked
1/4 c. bulghur wheat, uncooked
1/3 c. fresh parsley, snipped
1 c. shredded reduced-fat
    Cheddar cheese

Heat oil in a large skillet over medium heat. Sauté carrots and onions until tender. Stir in garlic and mushrooms; sauté for 3 minutes. Combine mixture with remaining ingredients except cheese. Spoon into a greased 2-quart casserole dish. Bake, covered, at 350 degrees for one hour, stirring once after 30 minutes. Top with cheese. Cover and let stand 5 minutes, or until cheese melts.

Slow down at meals...you'll eat less! It takes about 20 minutes after you start eating for your stomach to know it's full. Share the day's events with your family, listen to calming music or just think pleasant thoughts!

Mock Mashed Potato Bar

*Makes 6 servings at
180 calories each,
excluding optional toppings*

1 head cauliflower, broken into
   flowerets
1-oz. pkg. ranch salad dressing
   mix
2 T. low-fat milk
3 T. butter
1 T. garlic, minced

Optional: reduced-fat sour cream,
   reduced-fat shredded Cheddar
   cheese, chopped fresh chives,
   sliced black olives, crisply
   cooked turkey bacon, red
   pepper flakes

Boil or steam cauliflower until fork-tender, about 20 minutes. Drain in
a colander for at least 15 minutes, shaking several times. Transfer
cauliflower to a food processor; add salad dressing mix, milk, butter and
garlic. Process to the consistency of smooth mashed potatoes. Serve hot
with desired toppings.

Baked sweet potatoes are an easy side just about everyone will love. Bake at 375 degrees until tender, about 40 to 45 minutes. Garnish with a smidgen of butter and a dusting of pumpkin pie spice.

Lemony Broccoli

*Makes 6 servings at
80 calories each*

1-1/2 lbs. fresh broccoli,
   cut into spears
1 clove garlic, minced

2 T. olive oil
2 T. lemon juice

Add broccoli to a saucepan with a small amount of water. Cook over
medium-high heat for 6 to 8 minutes, until crisp-tender. Drain. Heat oil
in a small saucepan over medium heat. Sauté garlic to desired
tenderness. Stir in lemon juice; mix well. Pour mixture over broccoli,
tossing gently to blend.

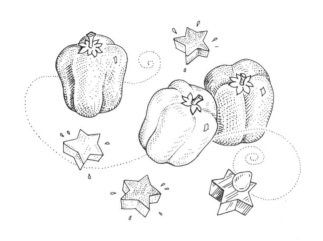

Use a crinkle cutter or mini cookie cutters to jazz up
zucchini, carrots, radishes and other sliced veggies for
salads, side dishes and appetizer trays.

Spicy Carrot French Fries

*Makes 6 servings at
130 calories each, excluding
optional salad dressing*

2 lbs. carrots, peeled and cut
    into strips
3 T. olive oil, divided
1 T. seasoned salt
2 t. ground cumin

1 t. chili powder
1 t. pepper
Optional: light ranch salad
    dressing

Place carrots in a plastic zipping bag. Sprinkle with 2 tablespoons oil and seasonings; toss to coat. Drizzle remaining oil over a baking sheet; place carrots in a single layer. Bake, uncovered, at 425 degrees for 25 to 35 minutes, until carrots are tender and golden. Serve with salad dressing for dipping, if desired.

Try adding a chicken bouillon cube to the water when
cooking vegetables, rice or pasta...you'll be surprised
how much flavor it adds!

Grandma's Wilted Greens

*Makes 4 servings at
70 calories each*

1 T. olive oil
2 cloves garlic, pressed
Optional: 1/8 t. red pepper flakes

1-1/2 lbs. fresh spinach, torn
1/4 t. salt

Heat oil in a skillet over medium-high heat. Add garlic and cook for
one minute, until golden. Add red pepper flakes, if using; cook
30 seconds. Add greens to skillet; sprinkle with salt. Cook, stirring
constantly, for 3 to 5 minutes, until greens are wilted. Serve warm.

If extra muffins are too tempting, freeze them! Muffins freeze well wrapped in heavy aluminum foil. To warm for serving, bake muffins, still wrapped, at 300 degrees for 12 to 15 minutes.

Carroty Bran Muffins

Makes 30 muffins at 120 calories each

2-1/2 c. all-purpose flour
2-1/2 c. bran flake cereal
3/4 c. low-calorie powdered
  sweetener blend for baking
2-1/2 t. baking soda
1 t. salt
2 c. buttermilk
1/3 c. unsweetened applesauce

2 eggs, beaten
1-1/2 c. carrots, peeled and
  shredded
1 green apple, cored and chopped
1 c. sweetened dried cranberries
1/2 c. chopped walnuts
1/4 c. flax seed

Mix together all ingredients in a large bowl. May cover batter and refrigerate up to 3 days, or bake right away. Fill greased muffin cups 2/3 full. Bake at 375 degrees for 15 to 18 minutes; do not overbake. Cool muffins; wrap in plastic wrap. Muffins will become moister if allowed to stand overnight.

No-sugar-added fruit spreads have all the sweetness of regular jam minus the calories. Use them to add a dollop of fruity flavor wherever you like...breakfast oatmeal, dinner biscuits, even stirred into vinaigrettes. Sweet!

Bran & Raisin Muffins

Makes 12 muffins at
130 calories each

2 c. bran and raisin cereal
1-1/2 c. low-fat milk
1-1/2 c. all-purpose flour
1 t. baking soda
1/4 t. salt

1 egg, beaten
1/4 c. low-calorie brown sugar
    sweetener blend for baking
2 T. butter, melted

Mix cereal with milk; set aside. In a large bowl, combine remaining ingredients; stir in cereal mixture. Fill lightly greased or paper-lined muffin cups about 2/3 full with batter. Bake at 350 degrees for 20 to 25 minutes.

Shh...here's the secret to flaky homemade biscuits!
Don't overmix or overwork the dough...just stir
to mix and roll or pat out gently.

Fluffy Whole-Wheat Biscuits

*Makes 12 biscuits at
110 calories each*

1 c. whole-wheat flour
1 c. all-purpose flour
4 t. baking powder
1/2 t. low-calorie powdered
   sweetener blend for baking

3/4 t. salt
1/4 c. butter
1 c. low-fat milk

Combine flours, baking powder, sweetener and salt; mix well. Cut in
butter until mixture resembles coarse crumbs. Stir in milk just until
moistened. Turn dough out onto a lightly floured surface; knead gently
8 to 10 times. Roll out to 3/4-inch thickness. Cut with a 2-1/2" round
biscuit cutter. Place biscuits on an ungreased baking sheet. Bake at
450 degrees for 10 to 12 minutes, or until lightly golden. Serve warm.

Make your own iced mocha beverage...so refreshing! Mix one cup brewed, chilled coffee, 1/2 cup low-fat milk, sweetener to taste and a teaspoon or two of sugar-free chocolate syrup. Pour over crushed ice in a tall glass and serve.

Crockery Parmesan Biscuit Bread

Makes 8 servings at 120 calories each

1-1/2 c. reduced-fat biscuit
    baking mix
2 egg whites, beaten
1/2 c. low-fat milk
1 T. dried, minced onion

1-1/2 t. low-calorie powdered
    sweetener blend for baking
1-1/2 t. garlic powder
1/4 c. grated Parmesan cheese

In a bowl, combine all ingredients except Parmesan cheese. Stir until a soft dough forms. Spray a 2-1/2 to 3-quart slow cooker generously with non-stick vegetable spray. Spoon dough into slow cooker; sprinkle with cheese. Cover and cook on high setting for one to 1-1/4 hours. Cut into wedges to serve.

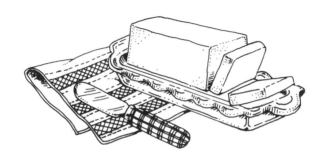

Substitute margarine for butter when baking, if you like.
Don't substitute reduced-fat spreads, though...they contain
more water than butter or margarine and will not give
the same baking results.

Salsa Roja

*Makes 12 servings at
45 calories each*

1 lb. roma tomatoes
2 T. olive oil
5 cloves garlic, chopped
1/2 c. onion, sliced and cut into
    very thin strips

1/4 c. serrano chiles, chopped
1 bunch fresh cilantro, chopped
2 T. lime juice
salt to taste

Arrange tomatoes on a broiler pan or a grill; roast tomatoes until skins
are blackened and tomatoes are soft. Set aside to cool. Heat oil in a skillet
over medium heat. Add garlic, onion and chiles; cook until golden. Place
all ingredients except salt in a bender and pulse to desired thickness. Stir
in salt. Cover and chill until serving time.

Salsa is flavorful, naturally fat-free and good on so many foods!
Try a spoonful of salsa as a topper for grilled chicken, burgers,
hot dogs or even baked potatoes...yum!

Sweet & Tangy Fruit Dip

*Makes 8 servings at
45 calories each; fruit not
included in calorie count*

1 c. fat-free cottage cheese
1/4 c. plain non-fat yogurt
2 t. honey
1 T. orange juice

2-1/2 T. low-sugar orange
marmalade
2 T. sweetened flaked coconut
fresh fruit slices

Place all ingredients except coconut and fruit in a food processor. Process
until smooth and creamy. Transfer to a serving bowl; stir in coconut.
Cover and refrigerate until chilled. Serve with a variety of fresh fruit.

Slip some fresh pineapple slices or ripe peach halves onto a
hot grill. The fruit will be hot and juicy in just a few minutes...
a sweet, tasty accompaniment to grilled meat,
or a scrumptious dessert on its own.

Bewitching Spinach Dip

*Makes 32 servings at
45 calories each; vegetable
slices not included in calorie count*

4 green onions
1/2 c. fresh parsley
10-oz. pkg. frozen chopped
    spinach, slightly thawed
8-oz. pkg. reduced-fat cream
    cheese, softened
3 T. dried, minced onion

1 c. reduced-fat cottage cheese
1 c. reduced-fat mayonnaise
1/2 c. reduced-fat sour cream
1/4 t. hot pepper sauce
1/4 t. pepper
1/4 c. lemon juice
assorted vegetable slices

Combine green onions and parsley in a food processor; pulse to chop.
Add spinach; continue to process until spinach has been finely chopped.
Remove mixture to a bowl; set aside. Without rinsing processor, add
remaining ingredients except vegetables. Blend until well mixed. Stir into
spinach mixture, blending well. Spoon into a serving bowl; chill several
hours before serving. Serve with vegetables.

Fill up a big party tray with crisp fresh veggies for dipping...
calorie-counting friends will thank you! Any extras can be
tossed into a crunchy salad the next day.

Easy Hummus Pinwheels

*Makes 80 pieces at
25 calories each*

15-oz. can garbanzo beans,
    drained
1 T. olive oil

2 t. ground cumin
1/4 c. green olives with pimentos
10 8-inch flour tortillas

Place all ingredients except tortillas in a food processor. Process on low
speed until well blended. Spread mixture evenly over tortillas. Roll
tortillas jelly-roll style; cut into one-inch pieces. Serve immediately, or
cover and chill for 2 to 4 hours.

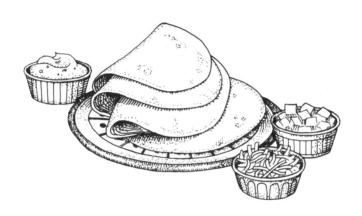

Try using colorful flavored wraps and tortillas for rollups...
sun-dried tomato-basil, garlic-herb or cilantro really give them
a zippy new look and taste without added calories.

Healthy Jalapeño Poppers

Makes 20 poppers at 35 calories each

1 T. olive oil
1/2 lb. ground turkey breast
3/4 c. green pepper, finely
    chopped
1/2 c. onion, finely chopped
1 clove garlic, minced

1/2 c. reduced-fat cream cheese,
    softened
Greek seasoning to taste
10 jalapeño peppers, halved
    and seeded
10 t. grated Parmesan cheese

Heat oil in a skillet over medium heat. Brown turkey with green pepper, onion and garlic; drain. Transfer turkey mixture to a bowl; blend in cream cheese and seasoning. Add one tablespoon of turkey mixture to each jalapeño half; sprinkle with Parmesan cheese. Transfer filled jalapeños to lightly greased baking sheets. Bake at 425 degrees for 15 to 20 minutes, or until tops are golden.

For a quick & easy snack that everybody loves, nothing beats a
big bowl of air-popped popcorn! Add flavor with a light sprinkle
of Italian seasoning and grated Parmesan cheese.

Apple Berry Salsa & Cinnamon Chips

Makes 8 servings of salsa & chips at 190 calories each

2 apples, peeled, cored and chopped
1 c. strawberries, hulled and coarsely chopped
1 to 2 kiwis, peeled and coarsely chopped

zest and juice of 1 orange, divided
2 T. brown sugar, packed
2 T. apple jelly

Combine fruit and zest in a large bowl. Mix juice, brown sugar and jelly in a small bowl; add to fruit and toss gently. Chill until ready to serve.

Cinnamon Chips:

6 8-inch flour tortillas, cut into wedges

2 T. sugar
1 t. cinnamon

Spray tortilla wedges with non-stick vegetable spray. Combine sugar and cinnamon in a plastic zipping bag. Place wedges in bag; shake to coat. Arrange wedges on a sprayed baking sheet. Bake at 375 degrees for 8 to 10 minutes, until crisp and golden.

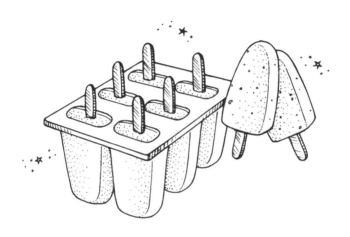

Whenever you drain canned or frozen fruit, save the juice.
Pour it into freezer pop molds and freeze for sweet
and healthy fruit pops.

Raspberry-Lemon Bars

*Makes 16 bars at
80 calories each*

3/4 c. plus 2 T. all-purpose
   flour, divided
2 c. no-calorie powdered
   sweetener for beverages,
   divided
1/8 t. salt
1/4 c. butter

1/2 c. egg substitute
1/2 c. half-and-half
1/2 c. lemon juice
1 T. lemon zest
1/4 c. reduced-sugar raspberry
   preserves

Mix together 3/4 cup flour, 3/4 cup sweetener and salt in a medium
bowl. Cut in butter until mixture is crumbly. Press dough into a lightly
greased 8"x8" baking pan. Bake at 350 degrees for 15 to 20 minutes,
until golden. Combine remaining sweetener and flour in a medium bowl;
mix well. Add egg substitute and half-and-half; stir until blended. Slowly
add lemon juice, stirring constantly; stir in zest. Spread preserves evenly
over warm crust. Gently pour lemon mixture over preserves. Bake at
350 degrees for 20 to 25 minutes, until set. Remove from oven; cool
completely. Chill for 2 hours before cutting into bars.

Oversize cookie bars are tempting, but for a change, slice them
into one-inch squares and set them in frilly paper candy cups.
Guests will feel free to sample "just a bite."

Light Pumpkin Cookies

*Makes 36 cookies at
80 calories each*

1 c. shortening
2 c. all-purpose flour
3/4 c. low-calorie powdered
  sweetener blend for baking
2 T. low-fat milk
1 T. unsweetened applesauce
1 egg, beaten

1 c. canned pumpkin
2 t. cinnamon
1 t. vanilla extract
1 t. baking powder
1 t. baking soda
1/2 t. salt

In a large bowl, combine all ingredients. Stir until well mixed. Drop by
teaspoonfuls onto greased baking sheets. Bake at 375 degrees for
8 to 10 minutes. Cool on wire racks.

Reduce the fat in a favorite recipe for cookies or quick bread.
Just replace all or part of the fat with unsweetened applesauce.
Canned pumpkin and strained prunes work well in brownie
recipes too...try it and see which one you like best.

Coconut Kisses

*Makes 24 cookies at
90 calories each*

3 to 4 egg whites
1/4 c. low-calorie powdered
   sweetener blend for baking
1/4 t. almond or vanilla extract

1/4 t. salt
14-oz. pkg. sweetened flaked
   coconut

In a large bowl, combine all ingredients except coconut. Beat with a wire whisk until frothy. Fold in coconut. Drop by tablespoonfuls, 2 inches apart, onto a parchment paper-lined baking sheet. Bake at 325 degrees for 20 to 25 minutes, until lightly golden, rotating baking sheet after 15 minutes. Cool completely; store in an airtight container.

Treat everyone to a heavenly light dessert. Spoon
juicy fresh strawberries, blueberries or sliced nectarines
into mini Mason jars and dollop with creamy vanilla
non-fat yogurt...luscious.

Harvest Pumpkin Mousse

Makes 4 servings at 100 calories, cookie topping not included

1-oz. pkg. sugar-free instant
  butterscotch pudding mix
1-1/2 c. low-fat milk
1/2 c. canned pumpkin
1 t. pumpkin pie spice

1 c. frozen whipped topping,
  thawed and divided
Optional: crushed gingersnap
  cookies

Whisk together pudding mix and milk for 2 minutes; let stand for 2 minutes, until softly set. Fold in pumpkin, spice and 1/2 cup whipped topping. Spoon into 4 dessert bowls; chill until serving time. Dollop each bowl with remaining whipped topping. Sprinkle lightly with crushed gingersnaps, if desired.

Serve up a light, cool fruit sorbet. In a food processor, combine
a cup of frozen fruit cubes, a few ice cubes and a teaspoon or so
of water. Process until smooth; add sweetener to taste
and serve immediately. Yummy!

Special Strawberry Pie

*Makes 8 servings at
110 calories each*

1 c. diet lemon-lime soda
.3-oz. pkg. sugar-free strawberry
   gelatin mix
1 T. cornstarch
3 c. strawberries, hulled
   and sliced

2 pkts. no-calorie powdered
   sweetener for beverages
9-inch pie crust, baked

In a small saucepan over medium heat, combine soda, gelatin mix and cornstarch. Cook and stir over medium heat until slightly thickened. Add strawberries; bring to a boil. Cool slightly; stir in sweetener. Spoon into baked crust; cover and chill until set. Cut into wedges.

Keep a notepad on the fridge to make a note whenever
a pantry staple is used up...you'll never run out of that
one item you need for your next healthy meal.

Fluffy Chocolate-Peanut Butter Mousse

Makes 8 servings at 150 calories each

2 c. low-fat milk
1.4-oz. pkg. sugar-free instant
    chocolate pudding mix
1/3 c. creamy peanut butter

8-oz. container fat-free frozen
    whipped topping, thawed
Optional: baking cocoa

Combine milk and pudding mix in a bowl. Whisk together until thickened and set; stir in peanut butter. Divide among 8 dessert bowls. Spread with whipped topping. Cover and chill for several hours, until firm. Garnish with a sprinkle of baking cocoa.

Make low-calorie desserts extra special with a pretty garnish.
Try fresh mint sprigs, curls of lemon zest, strawberry fans
or a dusting of cocoa.

Frozen Piña Colada Dessert

*Makes 8 servings at
150 calories each*

8-oz. container frozen fat-free
    whipped topping, thawed
3-oz. pkg. reduced-fat cream
    cheese, softened
1 T. no-calorie powdered
    sweetener for beverages

1/2 c. low-fat milk
8-oz. can crushed pineapple,
    drained and divided
1-1/3 c. sweetened flaked coconut

Spoon whipped topping into a bowl; set aside. In a blender, combine
remaining ingredients. Cover and process on medium speed for
30 seconds. Fold mixture into whipped topping; spoon into a freezer-safe
container. Cover and freeze until firm, about 4 hours. Let stand 5 minutes
at room temperature before serving. Return any leftovers to freezer.

INDEX

INDEX

Our Story

Back in 1984, we were next-door neighbors raising our families in the little town of Delaware, Ohio. Two moms with small children, we were looking for a way to do what we loved and stay home with the kids too. We had always shared a love of home cooking and making memories with family & friends and so, after many a conversation over the backyard fence, **Gooseberry Patch** was born.

We put together our first catalog at our kitchen tables, enlisting the help of our loved ones wherever we could. From that very first mailing, we found an immediate connection with many of our customers and it wasn't long before we began receiving letters, photos and recipes from these new friends. In 1992, we put together our very first cookbook, compiled from hundreds of these recipes and, the rest, as they say, is history.

Hard to believe it's been over 30 years since those kitchen-table days! From that original little **Gooseberry Patch** family, we've grown to include an amazing group of creative folks who love cooking, decorating and creating as much as we do. Today, we're best known for our homestyle, family-friendly cookbooks, now recognized as national bestsellers.

One thing's for sure, we couldn't have done it without our friends all across the country. Each year, we're honored to turn thousands of your recipes into our collectible cookbooks. Our hope is that each book captures the stories and heart of all of you who have shared with us. Whether you've been with us since the beginning or are just discovering us, welcome to the **Gooseberry Patch** family!

Jo Ann & Vickie

Visit our website anytime
www.gooseberrypatch.com

Email

Blog

You Tube

1·800·854·6673